CALLING HOME

SIMPLE AND POWERFUL PRAYERS FOR EVERYONE

LINDA SCHUBERT

Author of *Miracle Hour*

Resurrection Press
An Imprint of
CATHOLIC BOOK PUBLISHING, CORP.
Totowa • New Jersey

"Then you shall call, and the Lord will answer, you shall cry for help, and he will say: Here I am!" (Isa 58:9)

(T-RP768)

ISBN 978-1-933066-20-2

77 West End Rd.
Totowa, NJ 07512
Printed in USA
www.catholicbookpublishing.com

CONTENTS

Thank You even for the hard times in my life. Through the hard times You have strengthened me, and so I thank You for those times. When I am sick You teach me about wellness. When I am angry or depressed or in grief, You walk me through the murky waters to higher ground. You teach me about the power of the Holy Spirit, and how He helps me to pray. Your Spirit clears me to hear what I need to hear, and I am so grateful. My Spirit, united with Your Holy Spirit, is becoming soft and teachable. Your Spirit in me gives me discernment and power to turn from evil and toward good in all circumstances. You invite me to ask You questions, and You listen and respond, Precious Lord.

Lord, Your power in me enables me to change. I am rooted in love and growing in Your image and likeness. I am free to love. With Your Spirit in me I am able to recognize and seek help when I am out of control. I will not isolate myself when I hurt, but reach out for help in the Body of Christ. Thank You for the freedom, health, and joy this is bringing into my life. Jesus, You have come that I may have life to the full (see Jn 10:10), and I receive it now with gratitude. In Jesus' Name, Amen.

For today, tomorrow, and whatever the future holds, I return all of my life to You in peaceful and trusting surrender. Thank You especially for Your Son Jesus, my Savior and Lord. I belong to You, Lord Jesus. I love You. I am Yours forever. And I love to call Home. I pray in gratitude, in the name of the Father, Son, and Holy Spirit. Amen.

Blessing

May the God of peace sanctify you through and through. May you be transformed by the renewing of your mind. May you know that you were washed, you were sanctified, and you were justified in the name of the Lord Jesus Christ. And by the Holy Spirit may you always walk in the light and obey all that Christ reveals to you. May your heart be established in holiness. And may you be filled to the measure of the fullness of God. May He strengthen your heart so you will throw off everything that hinders and fix your eyes on Jesus. May you declare the praises of Him who called you out of darkness and into His wonderful light.

May you experience betrothal to our holy Lord and have depth of relationship with Him that makes all of heaven sing. And may you always know that you are loved, you are valuable, you are welcome. May you have the experience of truly being heard and understood. And may you know the precious power of the Holy Spirit always, in every area of your life. In Jesus' Name I pray. Amen. (*Precious Power*)

FOREWORD

Calling Home—Simple and Powerful Prayers for Everyone is a short but insightful reflection for beginners and those on the journey of growing in relationship through prayer. Our home is in the heart of God. It is where we came from and where we are going. But sometimes on the journey between the beginning and end points we become distracted and disorientated. Prayer allows us to reconnect with the source of our being, God who loves us unconditionally.

Each of the short chapters are meditations that will help one to reflect on important aspects of one's relationship with God. If we are not convinced that God loves us, it will be hard to connect with Him other than superficially. If we don't embrace the importance of forgiveness from the heart towards ourselves and others, our prayer will be sterile.

The need for a vision statement for this journey will help to keep our focus clear and our direction positive. In His love and mercy, God has poured forth the Holy Spirit to be our guide and teacher in this life journey we are on. His gifts are given to us to strengthen us in our response to the call of holiness and the call to mission.

As much as one may be afraid to make that call home to the Father, the Father desires to make it easy for us to do so. Sometimes we need a jump start. Ms. Schubert provides some simple jump starts that may help us to not only make the first response to God's invitation but to persevere on the call even in moments of silence. Ms. Schubert is truly a gifted writer. I hope that this will not be her last sharing with us.

Most Reverend Sam G. Jacobs
Bishop Emeritus
Diocese of Houma-Thibodaux

INTRODUCTION

Where is home to you? Home for me means safety and comfort. It's where I belong. I take off my shoes, curl up on the sofa, and connect with family and close friends. It's a place to regroup, restore, and renew. My Lord is Home to me.

AN INVITATION: In this book I am reflecting on the movement from awareness of the Lord in Heaven who we can call on, to knowing that He lives in us and is at home in us. In *Calling Home* we are inviting readers to acknowledge and grow in that intimate relationship. He and I are one, and that is where Home is. 2 Peter 3:18 says, "... *grow in the grace and the knowledge of our Lord and Savior Jesus Christ.*" In that established and growing relationship, it becomes easy for us to call Home, because it is where we belong. John's gospel Chapter 15 speaks of the vine and the branches. Jesus says in verse 4, "*Abide in me, as I abide in you. Just as a branch cannot bear fruit by itself unless it remains on the vine, so you cannot bear fruit unless you abide in me.*"

MOM CALLED HOME FOR ME: I recall a time when I was concluding a conference in Detroit, Michigan, all alone and heading through London to Lagos, Nigeria. I was in the airport, feeling tired, sick, and lonely. I really just wanted to go home and go to bed. I was too exhausted to call Home, so instead I called home (California) and spoke to my mother. I told her my situation, cried for help and asked for prayer. She prayed (called Home for me), and Father God answered. Things changed. I was empowered and ready for my next ministry assignment in Nigeria. The improvement I felt through her prayers was simple and powerful, and oh so real. The Lord in us and us in Him, rooted and established in love. I was filled up and ready to go.

Listen to this beautiful scripture in Ephesians. *"This is the reason why I kneel in prayer before the Father, from whom every family in heaven and on earth takes its name. I ask that from the riches of his glory he may grant through his Spirit that you be strengthened with power in your inner being, and that Christ may dwell in your hearts through faith. And I pray, rooted and grounded in love, you may have the power to comprehend with all the saints its breadth and length and height and depth, and know the love of Christ even though it is beyond knowledge, so that you may be filled with all the fullness of God"* (Eph 3:14-19).

OUR FOUNDATION: We need to know and remind ourselves that out of our Father's love for us, everything proceeds. We are rooted and established in love. This is our foundation, our home base. God the Son comes as our loving Savior to reveal and impart the character of God. We invite Him to be Lord of all areas of our lives. The Holy Spirit awakens faith in us. His work is to unite us to Jesus and enable us to live in Him.

CONNECTION MADE: When we agree to belong to Jesus, agree that He is our Savior and Lord, the connection is made. We are Christians, baptized into our heavenly home with Father, Son, and Holy Spirit. We are connected to our true Home. This is where we go when we pray. We pray to the Father, through Jesus, in the power of the Holy Spirit. He even helps us to pray. "*. . . even the Spirit helps us in our weakness. For we do not know how to pray as we should, but the Spirit himself intercedes for us with sighs that cannot be put into words*" (Rom 8:26).

PRAYER OF SURRENDER: Lord Jesus I come to You in humble trust and yield my life to You. I ask forgiveness for all the ways I have not honored You in my life. I turn away from sin and I turn to You. I believe in You, acknowledge You as my Savior and Lord, and receive everything You have given to me through Your life, death, and resurrection. Thank You for receiving me into Your family. I agree to belong to You. You are Home to me. In Jesus' Name, I pray. Amen.

AWESOME GOD: Father God I stand amazed that You would accept me in all my weaknesses and receive me with so much love. You come to us in humility asking, "What do you want Me to do for you?" (Mk 10:51). You speak tenderly even right now, as if to say, "Beloved, I know the wounds in your soul, but look to Jesus. Come to the light beyond the Cross. That light is my resurrection love that takes you beyond your wounds." Father, let the truth of Your love flow freely within me as I come to You now. Help me to feel the feelings I need to feel, but not be overcome or governed by them. Thank You, Father, in Jesus' Name we pray. Amen.

". . . that the God of our Lord Jesus Christ, the Father of glory, may give you a spirit of wisdom and revelation to know him. I further pray that the eyes of your heart may be enlightened so that you may know the hope to which he has called you, how rich and glorious is his inheritance in the saints, and how immeasurably great is the power that he has exercised toward those who have faith" (Eph 1:17-19).

I
Vision Statement

"For I know well the plans I have in mind for you, says the Lord, plans for your welfare, not for woe, plans to give you a future full of hope" (Jer 29:11).

NEED FOR CLEAR VISION: Precious child of God, have you thought about vision and purpose for your life? You know God loves you. You know He wants you to come to Him. Having clarity about your vision and purpose can make a huge difference in your life. I mean vision for you individually, for couples, and for things you are doing, projects, missions, etc., that reach beyond your own lives.

AN OPPORTUNITY: I remember a time when I was conducting a Catholic retreat in Dublin, Ireland. A disagreement emerged during a question and answer time about the different forms of, or approaches to prayer individually and in various groups. Some said we should always pray the Rosary. Others suggested various liturgical forms of prayer. We should do this. No, we should do that. Each one proclaimed what was right. Different ideas. No agreement. It seemed like a gathering without a purpose. I wondered what the Lord was bringing out of this retreat and wanted to be attentive to His plan. I finally asked if their groups had a vision statement—a clear focus of what they were about. They were clueless.

I contacted my friend Pat, leader of a prayer group in California called, "The Ephesians 1:4 Prayer Community," (to be holy, and blameless, and full of love), and asked him to fax me the vision statement for that group as a working model. We spent some time on the retreat reflecting on the process from the document. Then we began to define our purpose for that weekend retreat, and helped them take home some ideas and practical guidelines for their own groups. Much work was accomplished through developing an understanding of a vision statement. It was an empowering experience.

When I started Miracles of the Heart Ministries I wrote this vision and mission statement of purpose: Miracles of the Heart Ministries is dedicated to awakening Christians to the restorative power of God's love. Through the guidance of the Holy Spirit, Linda Schubert's goal is to provide resources that will bring healing and hope as we "*. . . grow in the grace and in the knowledge of our Lord and Savior Jesus Christ. To him be glory both now and for all eternity*" (2 Pet 3:18).

KNOWING WHO YOU ARE: So how does this relate to the purpose of this book? This is what I believe. There is something important about both knowing who you are and what the Lord is calling you to do. Whether you are married or single, you might seek the guidance of the Holy Spirit about His purpose for your life and ministry. Then write your own vision and mission statement for you as an individual or a married couple. Ministries or groups can do the same with great benefit. This clarification gives you strength and vision about your life and makes calling Home a natural thing—simple and powerful.

VISION PRAYER: **Thank you Father, for creating me, loving me, and giving me a vision for my life. I thank You that understanding of this purpose will unfold as I continue to trust in You and listen to You. You have plans for me, to give me hope and a future. I know I am to love and to serve and do what You put on my path to do.**

My life reflects Your presence living in me. You have chosen me, called me, and sent me with purpose and with unique gifts to help others. You have placed me in community to support and encourage me in accomplishing the assignments You have given to me. I listen to and respond to Your Holy Spirit. I accept and use the gifts You pour through me as I respond to Your call.

With Your grace I will walk the path You tell me to walk. With Your grace I will follow You despite obstacles, express Your love generously, forgive, bless, and heal. Thank You for the Holy Spirit at work in me now giving me hope and a wonderful future. I will check in with You (call Home) regularly and be confident that You always receive my call. Thank you, Lord. Amen.

"My soul proclaims the greatness of the Lord and my spirit rejoices in God my savior" (Lk 1:46-47).

II
Staying on Track

TAKE HOLD OF TRUTH: There are just a few things I want to touch on before we move to the next chapter. It's important to acknowledge that calling Home can be a problem for some people. When our birth home is not a safe or nurturing environment where our father or mother is not always a good parent, it's hard to freely and openly transition to calling Home to Father God. A shift needs to occur. Ask the Holy Spirit to help you look beyond your painful history and memories, and take hold of the truth that your true home is with God who will never harm you. The grace is present even now to do that.

AN AWESOME GRACE: I had an amazing experience in Jamaica once. I was conducting a "father blessing" service, and invited a few dads to come to the front and be stand-in fathers to pray a blessing for those coming forward. I learned later that one of the dads that came forward to be a stand-in father, in fact had a really bad relationship with his own father. But God's awesome grace took hold with that man, and as he prayed father blessings on those who came forward, the Holy Spirit poured into him, blessing upon blessing. It was life-changing for him.

So let's pray: Father God, some of my thoughts of home and parenthood have fallen short and don't reflect You. Come and cut away all false ideas of what home and parenthood is. I desire the warmth of a real home and a real daddy, so I fix my eyes on You. Give me the grace to call You Daddy.

YOU BELONG TO ME: Our awesome Lord is very patient and will work with us on clearing up the debris on the path. For example, my mother, a devout Christian, stepped off the Lord's path, got sidetracked, and dabbled in new age practices at an earlier time in her life. Then in an awesome moment of grace, the Lord spoke five life-changing words to her: "*Elizabeth, come out of there*." She listened, repented, and turned away from trying to change her life with unsafe and unhealthy practices. He was saying in essence, "You belong to Me, and it is My job to take care of you." She was restored to the intimacy the Lord wanted for her and for each of us. Is He telling you, "Come out of there"? He will help you find your way back Home. When you belong to Jesus He has amazing plans for you. When the path you walk with Him is clean and pure, His life can flow through you deeply and freely.

PRAYER: Lord Jesus, I repent of calling upon forces that are not centered on the power and work of the Holy Spirit. I renounce witchcraft

and all new age practices, everything that calls upon anything other than Your Spirit. With Your help I cut away all false ideas and programs that separate me from You. Cleanse me of all negative forces that block my true relationship with You. Refresh me in Your Holy Spirit. Thank You Lord. Amen.

RESOLVE: And then there is repentance. When I have conducted healing services that have a focus on repentance, all I can say is "Wow!" Our Lord loves having our path clean and clear so He can come in power. He loves us so much. Repentance means concrete recognition of our offenses, being genuinely sorry and determined to not sin again, asking for and receiving forgiveness, and if you are Catholic or belong to a sacramental church, it could include confession. We must resolve to take responsibility for our lives. *"Examine me, O God, and know my heart; test me and understand my thoughts. See if I follow an evil way, and guide me on the way to eternity"* (Ps 139:23-24).

THE POWER OF FORGIVENESS: Here are some steps I have offered during teachings on forgiveness (*True Confessions,* p.12).

1. Recognize the offense. Look at it and feel it.
2. Surrender the hurt to Jesus as a love offering.
3. Choose to forgive.

4. Ask Jesus to forgive them.

5. Ask Jesus to erase the memory of this offense.

6. Have compassion for the one who hurt you.

7. Receive healing for your vulnerability.

8. Go the extra mile. Bless those who hurt you.

9. Be grateful for the work accomplished and the work in process.

And, when you are struggling to forgive yourself, try instead to be open to God's forgiveness. His forgiveness is deep and lasting where your effort may be weak and transitory.

UNFULFILLED LONGINGS: We need to ask the Holy Spirit to show us areas in our lives that keep us from staying on track and prevent us from calling Home. Unfulfilled longings are the area where people tend to withdraw. This can be a critical danger zone. There are things we yearn for that aren't good for us, and they create blind spots. And there are things we crave that are healthy, God-given desires. People deeply desire acceptance and significance. Unsurrendered, these needs can lead us astray. Yielded to God, these needs are met in wonderful ways. As we give Him all of our cravings, our unfulfilled wishes, our unsatisfied needs, hopes, and hungers, He will bring us to a place of deep fulfillment (*True Confessions*, p. 27).

"To him who in all things is able through the power that is at work within us to accomplish abundantly far more than all we can ask or imagine, to him be glory in the Church and in Christ Jesus through all generations, forever and ever. Amen." (Eph 3:20-21).

III

Holy Spirit, Teach Me to Pray

THE FATHER'S LOVE PLAN: I am a convert to the Catholic Faith, with a history of wrong choices and wrong paths. Instruction in the Catholic Faith was exactly what I needed. I learned about the God of history, and our heavenly Father's wonderful love plan to restore people to fellowship with Him. I learned about the power of the Eucharist and reconciliation, and the ministry and work of the Holy Spirit. I eventually became involved in prayer groups in the Catholic charismatic renewal. Scripture became my daily food. My spirit was coming alive. I was getting in right order.

A MOMENT OF GRACE: The Holy Spirit was with me as I struggled with health issues, was diagnosed with breast cancer, and had a mastectomy. He put in my heart a yearning for a deep and meaningful life. One day in a blissful moment of grace I placed my hands on a world map and told the Lord I would go wherever He wanted me to go. In saying that, I stepped aside to allow the Holy Spirit to flow through me. It was a "Here I am, send me" moment. This released the Holy Spirit to do some amazing work in and through me.

LOVE AND TRUST: There are trust and love issues on the journey. The Lord wants us convinced that He loves us just as we are, no matter what we have done. He loved us before we were born and He loves us now; He will continue to love us no matter what we do. If we are certain we are loved by Him, we will be able to trust Him. When we trust Him we can entrust ourselves to Him and everything else of value. As we grow in relationship we will begin to know deep in our hearts that God is our loving Father. Home base becomes a solid reality.

HOLY SPIRIT POWER: When God asks us to do something He provides the power to do it. That power is the Holy Spirit, our enabler, the Spirit of Truth. To enable means to make us able to do something, to make possible, to equip. This is not passive acknowledgment but passionate participation. So we can thank Him for working in us to will and to act according to His good purpose (see Phil 2:13).

JOURNEY OF GROWTH: Fr. Robert DeGrandis, SSJ invited me to co-author books with him. This began an amazing journey of growth. Then after a family tragedy, I wrote *Miracle Hour*. Father DeGrandis believed in it and gave it a jump start.

Today I have traveled the world due to the popularity of *Miracle Hour*, the companionship of the Holy Spirit, and my willingness. I no longer travel due to health issues and age, but I ask the Lord to send my prayer books everywhere. Actually I told Him I still wanted to impact the world, but now from home.

CLEAR TO HEAR: Here is an important thought about the Holy Spirit. He helps us to be "clear to hear." It's really a gift. We learn to ask the Holy Spirit in circumstances that arise, "Lord, what should I do about this?" Then listen. "Lord, do you want me to go here?" Then listen. "Which way should I go?" Asking makes room for an answer. I spoke to my spiritual director, a Jesuit priest, about being "clear to hear." He responded, "That is truly Ignatian." He continued, "Along with clear to hear is step two, being free to act—asking for the grace to carry it out. You might hear the Lord say 'forgive,' and free to act means responding 'yes, I do forgive.'" Another thing he spoke of was being "in grace, or off grace." Trapped in fears of tomorrow, we are "off grace." Focused on now, we are "in grace." The grace is there to deal with now.

TONGUES AND MY SISTER: And then there is the Holy Spirit's gift of praying in tongues—heart-to-heart communication with Jesus. When I was baptized in the Holy Spirit I was released in the language of tongues. It has been an important part of my prayer life for many years. I want to share with you my deepest experience with tongues. My sister, Cherrill, was dying of ALS, Lou Gehrig's disease. She was a hospice nurse in Oregon and in a very deep crisis. One night, about 2 a.m., my niece Linda Sue called me from the hospital where her mom lay in the agonies of dying. I asked her to put the phone on speaker next to Cherrill's ear. Sitting on my bed I prayed, and yelled, and cried in tongues (calling Home from the depths of my being), and I heard my sister's wailing on the other end of the phone. It was excruciatingly painful, and yet so deeply holy and intimate in a way I will never forget. The next day my sister went home to Jesus. She had scribbled a note to my niece on a white board, because she couldn't talk, "I have to let go." I knew that our time on the phone helped pave the way on her journey Home.

A SPECIAL TREASURE: I heard an explanation from a Christian leader, that "tongues is a gift for the disciples of God. It's for those who want to grow and move on with the Lord." So I encourage you to be open about this gift of the Holy Spirit, which I believe is a treasure in helping Christians move on with the Lord in a deeper way. I have written a book on praying in tongues, because I believe it is a powerful way the Lord offers to guide us in calling Home. Most of my books have been "birthed in tongues" because I need the Lord's guidance in providing resources that will help build up the Body of Christ. When I pray in tongues I am "clear to hear." I'm not smart enough or wise enough to do it without Him. And I don't want to be.

DEPTH AND POWER: Pray: Lord, I believe throughout my life You have spoken to me. I haven't always heard You and the times I have heard, I haven't always trusted and obeyed. Yet You were there, drawing me closer. Today I have surrendered my heart to You at a deeper level and asked for the release of the Holy Spirit. I long for more of Your active presence and believe there is greater empowerment through praying in tongues, the language of the Spirit. Please release in me a special prayer language to communicate with You in increased depth and power. In humble trust, I give You my tongue and ask forgiveness for ways I have used it to hurt instead of to heal. Lord, bless my tongue and help me to freely yield it to You for prayer, praise, and a full range of expression. Teach me to pray. Thank You, Lord. Amen.

And as you quietly listen, He might say this to you: "Beloved, tell Me what is on your heart, but begin with a made-up language to loosen your tongue. Ask Me to form the sounds into your own personal prayer language, just right for you. Expect to feel My loving presence as you keep talking to Me in your special language. As you keep talking, expect Me to open fresh insights about your life and your unique needs."

LET'S REPORT FOR DUTY: Lord Jesus, by the power of your Holy Spirit, I give this day to You. I present myself to You to use in any way You choose. Assign me to serve as You wish. Use my mind, my voice, my hands, my heart. I will gladly share with others what You have done for me. I will share my life, my heart, my resources. I will lay hands on the sick and be an avenue for Your healing power. I will be courageous in walking where You ask me to walk and saying what You prompt me to say. When I hear Your voice I will say, "Yes, Lord," with a soft and open heart. I will be an instrument of reconciliation today. I will love, love, love. I will receive others in love and pray for them. Oh Holy Spirit, may each one I meet today be touched by the power of Your love flowing through me, revealing Jesus, my life. And when the day is over, I will return it all to You in gratitude as an offering of love. I will rest in Your power, Lord, and open myself so You can restore me and prepare me for the next day. (*Miracle Moments*)

"...and hope does not disappoint, because the love of God has been poured into our hearts through the Holy Spirit that has been given to us" (Rom 5:5).

IV

He is Waiting to Hear from You

SIMPLE AND POWERFUL: I want to make it easy for you to call Home, with simple and powerful prayers of the heart. We all face problems beyond our ability to resolve by our own strength. We all need answers. And we never outgrow our need to come to Him. Possibly now you feel more connected, centered, and maybe even a little needy. You love the Lord and He loves you, and He loves to hear from you. You can ask right now, if you want. With simple, childlike trust, just come to Him now. Or, you might ask, "Holy Spirit, what do You want us to talk about?" Then listen!

HE IS ALWAYS READY: I receive a variety of thoughts, and prayers, and ideas from people who read my books. One woman said, "There is no greater knowing for me than calling Home to my Father whenever I desire. He is always ready, willing, and able to help me." She continued, "Treasure this prayer time. Our Father loves to hear from us. Whether it is to repair our broken hearts, encourage us when we are weary, or when we do spiritual warfare. He equips us in battle through the Holy Spirit to destroy the works of the enemy." Another mentioned that her personal prayer time was her most valuable possession. She spoke of how our Father loves to hear from us, and that He stands ready like a soldier to protect and defend His children.

Here are some of the topics people expressed interest in including in this book:

* **Healing**
* **Acceptance of our state in life**
* **Remembering to call Home when things are on high speed**
* **Family inheritance issues**
* **How to pray in dry and difficult times**
* **Discerning His voice from your own thoughts**
* **How to pray in a bad marriage**
* **How to pray unceasingly**
* **Godly friends for children**
* **Moving**
* **New job**
* **Choosing a spouse**
* **Clarity in difficult situations**
* **Protection against the devil**
* **Addictions**
* **Peace in the storm**
* **To be still and hear**
* **For loved ones to know Jesus**
* **Family worship time**
* **Ability to receive**
* **Turning to Scripture for help**
* **Courage and faith to follow His direction**

* How to encourage those in endless struggles
* Resting in His love

And this, so important: Ensure that each day-to-day life choice goes through the filter of the Holy Spirit. These are treasured thoughts and insights, all coming from the hearts of Christians who spend time calling Home. I don't have answers, but I know the Lord loves, listens, and responds. I can help with "starter prayers" to suggest a track or framework for you to use and expand as you feel led in your own situation. Just be honest and real. Express your feelings, and make a decision to trust the Lord.

LOVED INTO REAL: Here is another thought that might help you. As I wrote in *True Confessions*, our deepest emotions have a childlike quality. Children are open, teachable, and trusting, free of intellectual hindrances and complicated motives. God wants to uncover hidden motives and barriers in our hearts and help us deal with them. Young children haven't yet learned to hide their feelings. They say what they feel and ask a lot of questions. Let's tell God what we feel and ask Him a lot of questions. If we don't ask Him, we tend to work in our own limited knowledge. *"...unless you change and become like children, you will never enter the kingdom of heaven"* (Mt 18:3).

My favorite children's story is *The Velveteen Rabbit,* a classic tale about a toy rabbit that is loved into becoming real. It loses fur and buttons from being loved and petted, but it becomes real in the loving. Jesus wants us to be "loved into real."

LET'S BEGIN: The hope is for you to get into the flow of the process, and move on from there. These are beginning prayers. An expanded step–by-step process is included in my book *True Confessions*. The steps include: getting in touch with feelings, inviting the Holy Spirit into the feelings, considering an example from Scripture, listening to what God might say, praying for others with similar needs, and then, no matter what, beginning to praise God.

Let's look at a few topics for prayer. It's all about love and humble trust. You can develop them further for your own situation as the Lord leads you.

1. **FEAR:** filled with apprehension, filled with concern or regret over situations, frightened, panicky, distrustful, dreading, anxious.

Reflection: I recall a time I was flying from San Francisco to Manila. My mind went into a downward spiral, as I was on assignment to present a seminar and didn't feel equipped. I was afraid. I figured they would find out how much I didn't know, and I would go home in disgrace. So I considered taking the first plane home. Then I heard the Lord saying strongly, "Rise up into who you are and fulfill the position I have given you." I sat up straight and said, "Yes Lord." The Lord knows your situation and has a plan to help you as He helped me on that ministry trip. Identify your emotions.

Prayer: Lord I just can't handle my situation. Things are out of control. This is happening:

____

____

____

____

____

Listen to what He might say: Beloved, remember, *"In love there is no fear, indeed perfect love casts out fear"* (1 Jn 4:18). I know you; I know what is going on; and I love you. Place your trust in Me. Let Me guide you step by step as you place your trust in Me. *"Do not worry about anything, but present your needs to God in prayer and petition, with thanksgiving. Then the peace of God which is beyond all understanding, will guard your hearts and your minds in Christ Jesus"* (Phil 4:6-7). *"Cast all your anxiety on him because he cares for you"* (1 Pet 5:7). *"Fear not, I am with you; be not dismayed; I am your God. I will strengthen you, and help you, and uphold you with my right hand of justice"* (Isa 41:10).

Response: Thank You, Lord. I place my trust in You.

2. **FAILURE:** Failure to perform a duty or expected action, falling short, lack of success, defeat, misfortune, tragedy, mistakes.
"In the time of trouble I call to you, for you will answer me" (Ps 86:7).

Reflection: In my earlier years I was in the habit of running away. I ran away from marriage more than once, and considered myself a failure in relationships with men. But as I came to know the Lord, He gently showed me how the pattern developed, and forgave me for my way of responding to situations. Once I heard in the silence of my soul, "You just haven't learned all I want to teach you." The Lord had so much love. Identify your emotions.

Prayer: Lord, I bring my list of failures to You.

____

____

____

____

____

Please forgive me and help me sort things out in a way that honors You.
Listen to what He might say: I love you, I always have and I always will. Receive My love into all those places where you feel like a failure. You are not a failure in My eyes.

Response: Thank You, Lord. I place my trust in You.

3. **PURPOSE:** End to be attained, intention, reason, prospect, aim, driving force, meaning.

Reflection: I recall a time after I was baptized in the Holy Spirit when I was longing for a life that was "meaningful and self-supporting." I was walking to Mass one morning, crossing a gas station parking lot, when I heard the voice of the Father, saying, "I will give this to you if you will use the freedom it gives you to honor Me." I wasn't exactly sure what "this" meant, but I continued to thank Him and trust Him for the future. That was many years ago, and I look back in gratitude for His working with me with so much love.

Prayer: Lord Jesus, I long for meaning and purpose in my life. I yearn for so much more.
Here is my list:

____

____

____

____

____

Listen to what He might say: Beloved, I created you with unique gifts. There is no one else exactly like you. Allow My gifts to unfold in your life as you place your trust in Me.

Response: Thank You, Lord. I accept my uniqueness, and I am open to the path You choose for me.

4. RELATIONSHIPS: Connections, affiliation, associations, companions, kinship, families, couples, attachments.

Reflection: So many people have asked me to pray for marriages, prodigal children, broken homes, and more.

Prayer: Lord Jesus, I bring my relationship situations to You. Here they are:

____

____

____

____

____

Listen to what He might say: Beloved, peace. *"A tranquil mind gives life to the body...."* (Prov 14:30). *"For he is our peace, who has made the two into one, by breaking down the barrier of hostility. In his flesh. . . ."* (Eph 2:14). Let Me bring you that peace as you place your trust in Me.

Response: Thank You, Lord. I rest in You.

5. COURAGE: Mental or moral strength to venture, persevere, and withstand danger; resolution, tenacity.

Reflection: When I was conducting a healing service in Poland, a 30ish white-haired man in the front row was watching me intently, holding on to my every word. During a break he came up to me and said, "Do you know why I love you, Linda?" (I didn't even know him!) He continued, "Because you have courage." I learned later that this man's parents had died in the death camp, Auschwitz, which we had visited earlier, and his father had left a note exhorting the living members of the family to trust the Lord.

Prayer: Lord, I want to have more courage in my life, especially in these areas:

____

____

____

____

____

Listen to what He might say: *"Be brave and steadfast; have no fear or dread of them, for it is the Lord, your God, who marches with you; he will never fail you or forsake you"* (Deut 31:6).

Response: Thank You, Lord. I receive Your courage.

6. WISDOM: Able to discern inner qualities and relationships; insight; marked by deep understanding and unusual discernment.

Reflection: More than anything in these challenging days, we need to ask for the Lord's wisdom. I find myself asking the Lord, "What should I do about this?" or, "How should I feel about that?" Then wait, listen, and in the quiet of your heart you will experience the movement of the Spirit to help guide you.

Prayer: Lord, I need Your wisdom, especially in these areas of my life:

____

____

____

____

____

Listen to what He might say: "*If someone among you lacks wisdom, he should ask God, who gives to all generously and without finding fault, and it will be given to him*" (Jas 1:5). "*Reflect on the Lord and his strength; seek his face continually*" (Ps 105:4).

Response: Thank You, Lord. I receive Your wisdom.

7. STRENGTH: Capacity for endurance; power to resist force; ability to confirm, establish.

Reflection: At one point in my life I read Scriptures on to a cassette that focused on a specific topic. Strength was one of the first ones. When I shared the tape with others, I was amazed to learn its powerful effect. People told me they even experienced deliverance from negative spirits when they listened to and absorbed all of the Scriptures on strength. *"Indeed, the word of God is living and active. Sharper than any two-edged sword, it pierces to the point where it divides soul and spirit, joints and marrow; it judges the thoughts and the intentions of the heart"* (Heb 4:12).

Prayer: Lord, I need Your strength in my life, especially in these areas:

____

____

____

____

____

Listen to what He might say: I am what you need. *"...find your strength in the Lord and in his mighty power"* (Eph 6:10).

Response: Thank You, Lord. I receive Your strength.

8. TRUST: Assured reliance on the character, ability, strength or truth of another; to have confidence in.

Reflection: I have traveled the world due to the popularity of my prayer book *Miracle Hour*. I have heard from people struggling with trust issues in South Africa, Nigeria, Poland, Malta, India, the Philippines, New Zealand, Australia, the Caribbean, around the USA and Canada, and more. And what continues to rise up in my spirit is this: If we really knew the Lord, really knew Him the way He wants us to know Him, trust would no longer be an issue. We belong to Him.

Prayer: Lord, I want to trust You. Please help me, especially in these areas:

____

____

____

____

____

Listen to what He might say: *"Trust in the Lord with all your heart, on your own intelligence rely not; in all your ways be mindful of him, and he will make straight your paths"* (Prov 3:5).

Response: Jesus, I trust in You.

9. HARMFUL HABITS

Reflection: Once when I was speaking to a group in Australia, I made the comment "Jesus is your self-control." Later I received a letter from a woman who heard that message. She wrote, "When you said 'Jesus is your self-control,' it went through me like a bolt of lightning. Since that moment I have not smoked one cigarette." As you pray for release from harmful habits or addictions, come to Him in humble trust. Remember it is in His timing and His enabling strength, not yours. Be set free!

Prayer: Lord, this is what I need release from:

____

____

____

____

____

Listen to what He might say: Beloved, I break the chains of alcohol, smoking, gambling, drugs, sex, unhealthy relationships. I am meeting the deep emotional, spiritual, and physical needs that provide a drawing power for these issues. I will be for you what you cannot do for yourself. I am pouring My healing into this area of vulnerability. Receive it from Me, with so much love. *"He reached down from on high and snatched me up; he drew me out of the watery depths. He delivered me from my powerful enemy, and from my foes, who were too strong for me. They assailed me in the day of my misfortune, but the Lord came forward to uphold me. He led me forth into the open field; he set me free because he was pleased with me"* (Ps 18:17-20).

Response: Lord, I am forever grateful. "*You will know the truth, and the truth will set you free*" (Jn 8:32).

10. GRIEF: A deep and poignant distress, a cause of suffering, sorrow.

Reflection: There are so many kinds of grief. In my situation, I have grieved so many deaths of people close to me that it would be hard to choose one example. I shared earlier the experience with my sister, Cherrill, and that will live with me forever. I also remember an extraordinary moment after my mother died. When I was in her Oregon cottage wandering around, I ran my hand over her favorite chair by a little wood stove. With a deep sigh, I cried out to God, "I don't want her to be gone, it hurts so much." Then the words from heaven flowed into my soul: "What if you knew how happy she was?" The place of pain became a place of worship.

Prayer: Lord, this is what I am grieving the most right now:

____

____

____

____

____

Listen to what He might say to you: Beloved, I lift you up. "*To place on those who mourn in Zion a garland instead of ashes, the oil of gladness instead of mourning. . . .*" (Isa 61:3).

Response: Lord, thank you.

11. FOR WHAT I AM STRUGGLING WITH THE MOST RIGHT NOW: Pain, anguish or distress, loss, jealousy, rejection, insecurity, illness, resentment, depression, sexual issues. Feeling stuck. What else?

Reflection: When God asks us to do something, He provides the power to do it. That power is the Holy Spirit. Our job is to believe in Him and let Him guide us through the various struggles. We can trust Him. Once in a time of mental confusion my mom prayed, "Lord, think through me today." Her thoughts were gently brought into right order. Our thoughts create emotions and affect our behavior. As we ask God for help, to "think through us," we gain control of our emotions. Without His help, the enemy will work in our minds to create a stronghold of wrong attitudes, desires, and thoughts. Every time we choose Jesus, our mind clears and the enemy loses power.

Prayer: Lord, this is what hurts the most right now:

____

____

____

____

____

Listen to what He might say: Beloved, call Home and tell Me about every detail of your situation. I am here, willing, ready and able to take you step by step through your situation. I love you, and I will work with you moment by moment as you put your trust in Me.

Response: Lord, I place my trust in You. Thank You for Your sustaining presence in all my situations.

V

When Tomorrow Comes

A WORD FROM MY MOM: As I write this, I am thinking about my mother, Elizabeth. I sat at her hospital bedside in North Bend, Oregon and heard her last "instruction" to me. She said, with fading voice, "Linda, always remember Philippians 4:19, '*...my God will fully supply all your needs out of the riches of his glory in Christ Jesus.*'"

This could be my last little book, and my heart is reaching out to you with that same Scripture. My voice isn't fading, but resounding with this word for you: As you continue on your journey Home, our Lord will meet all of your needs according to His glorious riches in Christ Jesus. As you turn to Him, moment by moment, in trustful surrender, you will find Him responding with a heart full of love and open arms.

OPEN TO HIS LOVE. Open your eyes to His love. Let Him burn away any residue of unlove. Keep your heart sweet and open. Reach for His hand firmly and say, "Jesus, I trust in You." Allow the Holy Spirit to reveal any deceptions that would cloud your relationship with Him.

Automatically turn away from anything that would take you away from Him. It isn't worth it.

Remember that you belong to Him, and it is His job to take care of you. Change will come; tomorrow is uncertain; but His goodness and mercy are accompanying you. You are safe in Him, and oh He loves you so much!

Entrust the process to Him, today and tomorrow. Remember to forgive with His forgiveness because all of His resources are yours. He is here to be your ability so come, take, receive from Him.

MORE FROM MOM. My mom left some treasures in her prayer journal. A choice one is this: "Self pity times must be kicked aside and the Lord's wisdom revealed." She continued, "It's hard to face ourselves sometimes, yet we must if living is to be vital. And I want a life with the Lord that is real and vital. Not religious in the wrong way, but real and clean."

Regarding her difficult marriage to my dad, mom said: "Jesus is so good not to have let either Charlie or me off the hook. I know real freedom comes from within, not from external circumstances. With this freedom comes more love and compassion for others." Through her journal one phrase was like a litany of God's faithfulness:

"Christ in you, the hope for glory" (Col 1:27). And when she stood at my dad's grave, she said, "Thank You, Lord, for teaching me how to live Your love."

GOD'S FAITHFULNESS. And so, my friends, I pray that we will be overwhelmed by the revelation of God's faithfulness, and His unending unconditional love and commitment—intimately, personally, in each of our lives. And I pray that we will absorb into our souls the revelation of His commitment to us so that we will deeply let Him have His way in us. That we will let Him live His life in us; that we are changed from glory to glory.

". . . that you may be filled with the knowledge of God's will through all spiritual wisdom and understanding. And we ask this so that you may live in a manner worthy of the Lord and become fully pleasing to him, bearing fruit in every good work and continuing to grow in the knowledge of God. May you be fortified with the strength that comes from his glorious power, and may you be granted patience and endurance, while joyfully giving thanks to the Father who has enabled you to share in the inheritance of the saints in light" (Col 1:9-12).

Let us say together: Thank You Father, for loving the whole world and loving me. Thank You for sending Jesus. Thank You, Jesus, for saying yes to the Father. Thank You for the grace to respond to His invitation to become a member of God's family—that I can call You Father, that I can be known as Your child. Thank You, Holy Spirit, for removing every barrier that would separate me from my Father.

GOD'S COMMITMENT TO US. Dear friends, we haven't even begun to realize how much He loves us. We must come back to the truth that His commitment to us is absolute. He is committed to love, protect, and guide us. He takes an amazing responsibility for a life fully surrendered to Him.

Father God, we receive Your life. Anoint each of us so that guided by Your power we can walk in the plan and mission You have chosen for us. In Jesus' name. Amen.

I will call Home. I will share with You my true feelings, needs, and desires. I will call Home.

". . throughout all these things we are conquerers because of him who loved us. For I am convinced that neither death, nor life, nor angels, nor principalities, nor present things, nor things to come, nor powers, nor height, nor depth, nor any other creature will be able to separate us from the love of God in Christ Jesus our Lord" (Rom 8

VI

More Prayers

Prayer of Gratitude

Father God, thank You for Your love. Thank You for loving me throughout my life, holding me close even when I didn't always recognize You. You loved me into life, and are helping me to stay on the path of loving and living. Thank You for helping me to draw closer and closer to You. Thank You for my family and friends and all those loving me and caring for me in times of need. Thank You for caring for them, protecting them, and helping them to know and experience Your love and mercy.

Thank You for all the ways You have helped me in my life. You have given me a vision for my life, focus, and purpose. You help me to see who I am, and who I belong to, and what life is all about. When I have wandered off the path, You drew me back with so much love and compassion. Thank You for the grace to keep my eyes on You as You call me closer. You taught me to take responsibility for my life under Your mantle of Love. Your Holy Spirit taught me how to surrender, repent, and forgive. I am so grateful.